MOVING TO THE UK

(from USA)

A simple **GUIDE OF 2021** for:

- **MOVING**
- **SETTLING** and
- **LIVING** in the UK.

Copyright © 2021 by Deena Kay

All right reserved. This book or any portion thereof may not be reproduced or used in any manner whatsoever without the express written permission of the publisher except for the use of brief quotations in a book review.

First Edition.

Disclaimer:

I am not a lawyer. The content provided here is simply for educational purposes and does not take the place of legal advice from your attorney. Every effort has been made to ensure that the content provided here is accurate and helpful for readers at publishing time. You are responsible for your own actions, choices, and results.

I know this book will save you every bit of trouble while moving to the UK and starting a life there. If you find the information useful, I am happy about that, and you are welcome to refer it to someone who needs it.

Thanks for your support! Now let's read.

TABLE OF CONTENTS

MOVING TO THE UK 1

GETTING STARTED 6

#1 VISA REQUIREMENTS & JOBS 6

#2 COST OF BILLS 14

#3 APARTMENT RENTING 15

#3 HEALTH SERVICE (NHS) 22

#4 INSURANCE 24

#5 BANKING 25

#6 PHONE NUMBER 30

#7 NATIONAL INSURANCE 31

#8 DRIVING LICENCE 32

#10 IMPORTANT WEBSITES 36

#11 DEDUCTIONS FROM YOUR PAY 38

#12 GROCERIES AND SHOPPING 42

#13 SELF-EMPLOYMENT 44

#14 PEOPLE AND LIFESTYLE 46

#15 TRANSPORTATION 48

MOVING TO THE UK

Prepare for moving.

So the time has come. At this moment I imagine you are serious about moving or maybe you are not entirely sure about it, and you want to have as much information as possible. Whatever it is, you wouldn't read this right now, if you haven't give it a good thought about it at least.

I realize this is a huge step (forward I guess) and only those of us who have already experienced it, know the struggle it brings. I couldn't find a guide like this when I was moving which made things so much more complicated for me for I had to learn everything the hard way.

Why do I want to help you?

Our experience of moving wasn't nearly as simple as I thought it would be but rather exhausting. All the trouble was worth it after all but if I had found a detailed guide at that moment that would provide me with all the information I needed, my six months of moving and settling down would be so much better. And this is coming from a tough woman, a woman who can handle just about anything.

That is why I decided to help you go through it a lot more easily. It took me months to gather all of the information. And time is a valuable thing to all of us. Lately, time is *the* most valuable thing to me.

Not to mention spending the amount of my entire monthly food budget because of long telephone calls. Imagine calling five different offices daily to get information and most of the times the discussions on the phone were very long. Oh, and those waiting lines, you know these, right? Calling from another country can cost you all right.

That is why I created this short but helpful guide in such a simple way so I don't complicate your life even more.

What to take care of before moving?

Turning into a minimalist would probably be the first thing that comes to my mind before moving. Why did I mention this first? Let's say I've moved quite a few times in my life and dragging non-important, never-been-used things (or should I say junk?) from one flat to another is exhausting. You want to move with as little stuff as possible. Trust me, less is more!

It's probably the best if you get rid of everything you don't *really* need. One of the reasons why I believe you should become a minimalist is guilt. You probably feel guilty because a lot of your things don't serve their purpose (or don't have any purpose at all). Somebody else will be happy to have them. So give them away. I started with small things like accessories, toys, the old guitar I didn't use anymore, sports equipment I overgrew, plates, mugs and many, many clothes. Maybe I will still wear it someday, I said to myself. But I never did. Until the time came and I gave away half of my clothes. Do you want to know how I felt after?

Relieved. And free from all the burden.

I would love to tell you 'rent a van and make a road trip to the UK, if possible. We did. It was fun, and all our stuff could fit inside a van. We only had to drive once.' But unfortunately, I cannot say that. You cannot rent a van when moving overseas. When you move from US.

The shipping costs a fortune. So it is best if you could sell as much as you can before moving. We did! It is better to buy new or used things after you find an apartment to live in. It's not 'just' the cost but the idea of starting fresh is also very attractive. New life, new things, new start.

There are a few things to consider when you're deciding what to bring over from the US. Anything that has a motor or a heating element (coffee machines, blenders, etc.) usually only works on one voltage (120V in the US). So, your air fryer and Nespresso machine probably won't work on UK voltage. You'll need to look around on the appliance to see what voltage it's rated for (usually it's on the bottom or near where the cord goes in).

Although you could technically buy a transformer to step down the UK voltage, they put a lot of wear and tear on the appliance and aren't the safest things to use.

Shipping overseas is really expensive (have I already mentioned that? :)), and the UK income tax rates are pretty high compared to the US.

So let's get to the point. How to move overseas?

Flights from the UK (London) to other countries and vice versa are very affordable and regular. London airports are super connected with the rest of the world so finding a good flight should be the last worry on your mind. Maybe not in the time of pandemic but in general, this is the case. When looking for flights, I recommend checking Skyscanner to compare flights.

Transferring money to the UK from the US

Before you cross the Atlantic for a new life in the UK, you'll probably need to convert some of your savings into British pounds.

Try to avoid using high street banks for this process because of their high fees, and you won't get the best exchange rate.

Luckily, there is one super easy solution. It is called **Wise** (previously called TransferWise). There are other of course but this is the one I recommend and I can say for sure everyone else will. So if you need to pay anything in advance, sign up for the Wise account. It will be so much simpler and cost-effective than an international wire transfer from your bank, I promise! You can even open a Wise Multi Currency Account, which lets you send and receive money in over 40 currencies.

So let's get to the main starting point. Getting that visa, shall we?

"All mankind is divided into three classes: those that are immovable, those that are movable, and those that move."

-Benjamin Franklin

GETTING STARTED

#1 VISA REQUIREMENTS & JOBS

You can skip this part if you already have a job or know exactly what you want to do and how to manage it and you don't need my help. If that is not the case, please continue reading.

Any US citizen moving to the UK will need to obtain a visa which can take weeks to months. It all depends on the circumstances. It's illegal to work in the UK on a tourist visa (including as a digital nomad -sadly), or even go job hunting, and getting caught will likely result in both deportation and a permament ban.
Yes, the UK has become increasingly strict about immigration now that Brexit has passed. It's quite a difficult country to move to as an American. But there are options if you're willing to put in the effort.

Your best options are and I am not gonna lie - these are the most common ways to get a UK resident visa as an American:

- **Marry a UK citizen**
- **Attend college or university in the UK**
- **Get hired and sponsored by a UK company**
- **Transfer to a UK office within your current company**
- **Possess exceptional talent or promise in a desirable field**

This is not an entire list of UK visa opportunities. I highly recommend reading the UK goverment page on visas and immigration to fully understand your options and the requirements for each visa type. Some visas, like the Tier 4 Student Visa or Tier 2 Intra-Company Transfer Visa, have no path to citizenship, so do your research.

First, let's make it clear that the UK allows citizens of many countries to enter without a UK visa and stay for a max of 6 months.

If you're from United States or one of these countries -

>Andorra, Antigua and Barbuda, Argentina, Australia, Bahamas, Barbados, Belize, Botswana, Brazil, Brunei, Canada, Chile, Costa Rica, Dominica, East Timor, El Salvador, Grenada, Guatemala, Honduras, Hong Kong, Israel, Japan, Kiribati, Macau, Malaysia, Maldives, Marshall Islands, Mauritius, Mexico, Monaco, Micronesia, Namibia, Nauru, New Zealand, Nicaragua, Palau, Panama, Papua New Guinea, Paraguay, St Kitts and Nevis, St Lucia, St Vincent and the Grenadines, Samoa, San Marino, Seychelles, Singapore, Solomon Islands, South Korea, Taiwan, Tonga, Trinidad and Tobago, Tuvalu, Uruguay, Vanuatu and Vatican City

- **then you are good to go.**

Also, the citizens of British Overseas Territories and the citizens of Commonwealth countries born before 1 January 1983 who qualify for Right of abode (ROA) through a parent being born in the UK also have the right to enter UK without a UK visa and reside with no need of UK residence permit.

So you should really check if you meet any of the criteria mentioned above.

Citizens of all other countries will require a UK visa to enter the UK. You can check exact UK visa requirements on the UK Visas and Immigration od the UK government site.

There are many types of visas, but I'll only cover a few types of **work visas**, that are most certainly relevant to you.

Tier 1 (Exceptional Talent) visa – a UK work visa for those recognised as leaders in science, humanities, engineering, medicine, digital technology and the arts. This needs to be endorsed by the UK Home Office and only 1,000 of these visas are issued each year. It is valid for up to 5 years and can be extended for another 5 years.

Tier 2 (General) visa – a UK work visa for those who have been offered a skilled job (annual salary of at least £25,000) and have been sponsored by licensed organisation related to their employment. It is valid for up to 6 years.

Tier 2 (Intra-company Transfer) visa – UK work visa for those whose overseas employer has offered them a transfer to a UK branch, on condition of sponsorship. The visa can be valid for between 6 months and 9 years, depending on the position offered.

Tier 2 (Minister of Religion) visa – UK work visa for those who have been offered a job within a faith community, on condition of sponsorship. The visa is valid for up to 3 years and can be extended.

Tier 2 (Sportsperson) visa – UK work visa for elite sportspeople or qualified coaches endorsed by their sport's national governing body. The visa is valid for up to 3 years and can be extended for a further 3 years.

Tier 5 (Temporary Worker) visa – UK work visa for those engaging in temporary work as a charity volunteer, sports person or creative worker, religious worker, on a government authorised exchange or as part of an international agreement, providing sponsorship has been secured. The temporary UK work visa is valid for between 1 and 2 years, depending on the purpose.

Tier 5 (Youth Mobility Scheme) visa – UK work visa for those aged 18-30 from Australia, Canada, Japan, Monaco, New Zealand, Hong Kong, South Korea or Taiwan who have at least £1,890 in savings. The visa is valid for up to 2 years.

Domestic Workers in Private Household visa – UK work visa for private domestic workers who have worked for their employer for at least a year. Valid for a maximum of 6 months.

Note that there are so many types of visas (work visas and other types) there should be a seperate book to cover each of them in detail. I stopped counting, honestly.

So I suggest you check them all at https://www.gov.uk/browse/visas-immigration/work-visas and see if you fit into any of the category or if there is a specific visa you're interested in.

UK visa fees:

If you're a skilled worker who's earned a job with one of the countless approved companies in the UK, you can apply for a Tier 2 general visa from three months before your start date.

Need to stay for up to three years? It'll cost you £610 to apply, plus another £610 for each of your dependents (family members, basically.)

Want to make the UK your home for more than three years? The cost doubles to £1,220 ($1,488,) plus – yes, you guessed it – another £1,220 ($1,488) for each of your dependents. For a family of five, that means spending £6,100 ($7,440) for the right to live in the UK.
In either case, **it's 15% more expensive to apply for the visa from inside the UK**.
You'll also have to pay **an Immigration Health Surcharge of around £800 ($976)** for you and each of your dependents.

You can always check for your UK visa costs here: https://www.gov.uk/visa-fees

In general, you'll get most of the information needed, right here: https://www.gov.uk/government/publications/usa-apply-for-a-uk-visa/apply-for-a-uk-visa-in-the-usa

Apply for a UK work visa

The documents you will need to provide, depend on the type of UK work visa you are applying for.

But in general, make sure to get the following documents:

- A certificate of sponsorship from your employer
- Proof that you're being paid the "appropriate rate" – usually at least £30,000 ($36,600) per year
- A bank statement showing you have had £945 in your account for 90 days before your application
- Evidence showing you are able and allowed to travel
- Your travel history over the past five years
- proof of English language ability
- proof of payment of the healthcare surcharge

After you've collected and prepared all of this information, be ready to visit a visa application centre to get your fingerprints taken and your photo taken for a biometric residence permit.
100% of New York-based applicants for this visa get an answer within 30 days, but it doesn't usually take that long. **Half the people get a response within two days, and 99% get a reply within 15 days**, according to the UK government.
Remember to collect your biometric residence permit within 10 days of when you wrote that you would arrive in the UK.

You can either apply at the UK visa application centre in your country, or you can apply online through the UK Home Office Visas and Immigration Service website:
https://www.gov.uk/apply-uk-visa

Applying for a Biometric residence permit
Citizens from non-EU/EFTA countries who want to stay in the UK for longer than 6 months need to apply for a UK biometric residence permit (BRP). The BRP is valid for the duration of your stay in the UK, up to a maximum of 10 years.

You can apply for a UK biometric residence permit from inside the UK at a post office or Visa premium service centre, or from outside the UK at a UK visa application centre. A list of Visa premium service centres in the UK can be found on the following link:

https://www.gov.uk/ukvi-premium-service-centres/find-a-premium-service-centre

Residents can apply for a permanent residence permit or full UK citizenship after living in the UK for 5 years.

There is a variety of job opportunities in the UK.
Most common websites for job search are Linkedin and Indeed. Create a Linkedin account, start networking and applying for jobs.

Work-life balance.

Chances are that you'll have a great time working in the UK. The country was ranked among the 10 highest in the world for workplace happiness in 2019. The employment rate is also very high - above 75% which is really good.

People are usually working Monday-Friday 9 AM - 5 PM. The traffic is terribly dense. The public transport is also extremely crowded. It is best if you walk by foot or drive a bike if your workplace is not too far away from your apartment.

In the UK, it seems like life is all about work. Not a quality lifestyle but it is all up to you in the end. It is completely possible to have a great work-life balance if you know how to manage your time more efficiently.

What kind of salary can you expect on average?

I've taken this average from few largest cities in the UK. It will give you an approximate idea of how much you can expect to be paid.

City	Average annual salary
London	$43,467
Edinburgh	$34,931
Glasgow	$32,316
Belfast	$30,275

Jobs in the UK for students

The UK is an excellent country to attend university. Not only do Cambridge and Oxford occupy the top two spaces in the Time Higher Education's World University Rankings, but London alone has four institutions in the top 40.

To study in the UK, you need to apply for a Tier 4 general student visa. You can do this from three months before your course is set to start, and should get a decision within three weeks of sending off the application.

Before you apply, make sure you:
- Have been formally offered a place on a course at a UK university
- Can speak, read, write and understand English
- Have enough money to pay for your course and support yourself

And get together the following documents:
- A valid passport or other valid travel document
- Evidence you can support yourself and pay for your course
- Proof your legal guardian consents to you getting the visa, if you're under 18
- Proof of your relationship with your legal guardian, if you're under 18

It costs £348 to apply for this visa from outside the UK. You must pay an additional £348 per person for each dependent you want to come

over with you. You'll also have to pay an **Immigration Health Surcharge of around £1,000 ($1,220).**
If you're successful, you can come over to the UK a month (or less) before your course starts.

#2 COST OF BILLS

Compared to US your monthly expenses for bills will probably drop a little bit, which is good news.

As you can see below, is again an approximate cost of bills for the UK and the US. Internet is very cheap. We have a high speed internet because I work online from home all the time and we only pay around $25 for it. Our internet provider is TalkTalk (in case you're interested).

Bill (monthly)	UK	US
Gas and electricity	$118 (USD)	$175 (USD)
Water	$40 (USD)	$38 (USD)
Internet	$21 (USD)	$44 (USD)
Income tax for average wage (including federal taxes)	20%	22%

The highest of all bills is a council tax. Every household has it and you cannot avoid it. The cost of it depends on the value of the property you're in, on number of people in your household, and of course the region you're living in. We live in Nottinghamshire (1-bedroom apartment for a couple) and pay a little bit over 100 GBP for a council tax.

#3 APARTMENT RENTING

First, let's say a quick few words of the cheapest options before finding your own apartment.

There is always a possibility to stay in a hotel or a hostel, but I wouldn't recommend either of those. The first one is too expensive, and you can't prepare your own meals which makes it an even higher expense.
Eating out in the UK isn't something you want to do if you want to save some money because it's going to cost you a lot.

Except you aren't looking for healthy meals. Fast food is always a cheap deal if you don't mind eating it. So back to the 'where to stay' part...

Hostels are the cheapest option out there but if you want to have good quality sleep, prepare your meals (and not get robbed), do not stay there.

So the best and most affordable choice (if you count the food expense) from our experience is to **stay in Airbnb**. You basically have your room or an entire apartment, use of kitchen, bathroom in someone else's home in exchange for a low price. We always stay in Airbnbs when traveling around. It's the best option you can find.

Now, how about that apartment of yours?

Rent pricing in UK is definitely something you should look into when searching for the right location. The difference in price between one region and another can be huge so let's dive into the details. The following table will show you the average monthly rent for each UK region.

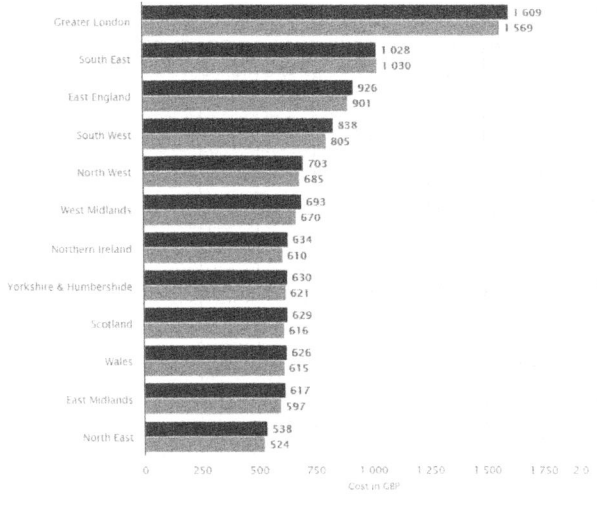

We moved to Nottinghamshire which is in East Midlands area. As you can see, it is a part of the UK with a very low property cost. This has also helped with our decision to move there. And because it is a nice city and close to the Lake District National Park. It is also quite famous for Robin Hood.

Clearly, you can find a place with much lower rent than average anywhere in the UK, even in London but you should also be careful of the state in which apartment is in.

For instance, you can easily find a room in London within a shared flat for 400 GBP. But don't expect it to look good. Right on the contrary.

As we all know pretty well, UK is a rainy country and many apartments are unfortunately affected by damp and mould.

Not something we want but there it is, quite common in the UK. It is difficult to get rid of it, and it smells bad, not to mention a terrible effect it has on your health. So be careful when renting a place. Take a look at every spot, especially behind the furniture.

I hope you'll never have to deal with something like this in your life. We have because we didn't know when we moved into apartment that it had damp issues. It was renovated and we weren't paying attention to details.
We learned our lesson the hard way. After having to throw away half of our clothes. And moving to another apartment because it's not humanly acceptable to live in the place with such damp problems.

I really don't have to stress this but when you rent a flat, it is advisable to make a contract with your landlord - **tenancy agreement**.

This agreement has to include yours (as a tenant) and landlords rights and responsibilities. The tenancy can either be fixed-term (for a set period) or periodic (week-by-week or month-by-month basis).

For more information on renting rights and responsibilities, visit this website: https://www.gov.uk/private-renting

Rental fees that can occur before you move in:

Holding deposit
Potential cost: £200-£500
This is a sum charged by the lettings agent to 'reserve' the property and take it off the market. The amount varies but one weeks' rent is a good benchmark. However, as the amount is subtracted from your main deposit (between four and six weeks' rent) which is returnable, a holding deposit is not really a fee.

You'll only lose the money if you don't proceed to signing the agreement after the property has been taken off the market.

Contract/ administration fee
Potential cost: £350
This fee covers drawing up the contract (usually an Assured Shorthold Tenancy agreement) as well as any other administrative tasks such as the inbound inventory, phone calls and photocopying.

*WE DIDN'T HAVE TO PAY THIS FEE.

Reference checks
Potential cost: £75-£100 per person
This pays for the agent to run references on you and anyone else named in the contract. They'll usually contact your current employer and/or previous landlord. If you are using a guarantor, they'll be referenced too.

*WE DIDN'T HAVE TO PAY THIS FEE.

Credit checks
Potential cost: £50-£100 per person
This pays for the lettings agent to conduct a credit check on you using a credit reference agency such as Experian or Equifax. Even if just one of you is responsible for paying the rent, the agency may still credit check both of you.

*WE DIDN'T HAVE TO PAY THIS FEE.

Once you're in the property:

Tenancy renewal
Potential cost: £150-£180
This pays to renew your contract at the end of the tenancy agreement should you choose to stay on at the property. This is also the time at which the landlord is at liberty to put the rent up.

Amendment to contract

Potential cost: £100-£120

This could be payable if you require the existing contract to be amended. For example, you want to change the term or swap a housemate.

Unpaid rent
Potential cost: Around £30 per payment

You will need to set up a standing order, so your rent comes out of your bank account directly. However, if there's not adequate funds and the payment bounces, your lettings agent or landlord may charge you (your bank might too).

Early termination
Potential cost: Up to £300 per person

If you want to leave before the tenancy agreement ends and your landlord doesn't agree on it, not only will you be liable for the outstanding rent, you could be hit with early termination fees too.

When you're checking out:

Check out fee
Potential cost: £100-£300

This will pay for the outbound inventory, where the agent will check everything is in order with the property when you leave and that it's been cleaned to the appropriate standard.

Deposit deductions
Potential cost: Up to the cost of your initial deposit

If the lettings agent finds any damage to the property or any items missing from the inventory, they could deduct the cost from your deposit.

5 documents your landlord must hand over to you (by law)
1. A copy of the Government's rental guide

This guide sets out all the information you should be given as tenant, your legal rights and what to expect from the rental process: **How to rent: The checklist for renting in England**:

https://www.gov.uk/government/publications/how-to-rent

2. A gas safety certificate
If your rental home has any gas installations (such as an oven), your landlord must arrange an initial gas safety check as conducted by a Gas Safe engineer – and provide you with a certificate. If they don't, you can report them to the **Health and Safety Executive** (HSE).

3. The paperwork protecting your deposit
Your landlord must hold your deposit in a government-backed Tenancy Deposit Scheme, so you'll be protected if there are any disputes at the end of the tenancy. You'll be given the paperwork for the scheme which should clearly state the sum being held.

4. An Energy Performance Certificate (EPC)
This certificate rates the energy-efficiency of your rental home, from A (most efficient) to G (least efficient).

5. Relevant contact details
Your landlord (or lettings agent acting on behalf of the landlord), should provide their full contact details including address and telephone number in case of an emergency.

A 'nice-to-have'...
It's not law, but it's good practice for your landlord to provide you with reports of any electrical inspections.

You may also check other websites when looking for an apartment or house. I personally recommend Rightmove and Zoopla.

You can also search for property on Gumtree but it's not the most user-friendly website. We usually use Gumtree for buying and selling second-hand. See for yourself.

#3 HEALTH SERVICE (NHS)

The UK's health system ranks highly on a global stage, all while costing the taxpayer a fraction of what people usually have to pay in other countries. Your healthcare will be, therefore, mostly free (if I can use the word free when nothing is actually free).

After you pay the Immigration Health Surcharge included in your visa application, you'll be able to use the National Health Service (NHS).

Compared to the nightmare that is the American healthcare system, the UK's National Health Insurance (NHS) is a ray of sunshine. I'd say it's one of the best things about living in England. The system isn't perfect, but it does provide healthcare to all residents, regardless of their employment status.

Nearly all medical services and treatments are free, with the exception of certain things like prescriptions and dental procedures. The bad news is that dental procedures are ridiculously high in the UK as well. And even those are far cheaper than what you'd typically pay in the US with an average employer insurance plan.
Although, most people who move to the UK will need to pay the immigration health surcharge when making their visa application, as it was mentioned already. The amount you have to pay depends on your visa type and your length of stay.

Waiting times can vary and sometimes last months, but the NHS has an excellent reputation, from its GPs to the operations it performs – plus it's free.

Private medical cover has its advantages though – providing you can pay.

You'll also be funding the NHS through your taxes. The amount of money you'll pay in UK taxes will likely be much higher than what you paid in the US. Despite the lower pay, it is better to live in a country where people aren't filing for bankruptcy because their child was diagnosed with cancer. That's my point of view.

It's time to get your unique NHS Number (NHS stands for National Health Service) and find yourself a General Practitioner (GP), in other words, a doctor.

Look for a GP near your address which you can do here:
https://www.nhs.uk/Service-Search/GP/LocationSearch/4

Just enter your address to find and compare local practices in your area.

Choose one and pay a visit to one of the local practices. Just make sure to bring a copy of your passport and a letter of address with you (they have to see where you live).

Now, you wait for a NHS Number which you will receive in a few weeks to your address.

If you want to learn more about NHS Service, make sure to visit this
https://www.nhs.uk/nhsengland/aboutnhsservices/

#4 INSURANCE

In case you need any insurance whether it is private health insurance, travel insurance, car insurance, home insurance, pet insurance, etc. It is best explained on Compare the Market (comparethemarket.com)

I strongly recommend this website since insurance is a very broad topic. All I can say currently is that a car insurance can be quite expensive so think carefully about buying a suitable car for you. In other words, do the math. See how far can you go with your monthly expenses.

We are currently using Admiral car insurance and so far we're pretty satisfied with their low cost compared to others out there. Although we have a small economic car, the price of £50/month is still reasonable.

*I'll also add all essential website links in a separate chapter.

#5 BANKING

Once you move, choosing the right bank for you is also one of the first things you need to take care of. I am not going to complicate this section too much.

All I will do here is show you the list of most common traditional banks in the UK, introduce you to the non-traditional banks all of us use and why we will never go back to traditional banking anymore.

If you're more of a traditional type, you might want to consider choosing a bank from the following list.

- **HSBC Holdings**
- **Barclays**
- **Lloyds Banking Group** - Includes **Lloyds Bank** and **Bank of Scotland**
- **Royal Bank of Scotland Group**
- **NatWest**, the **Royal Bank of Scotland** and **Ulster Bank**.

Whatever you select, the procedure is usually the same. You have to **make an appointment** to open your bank account. But do note that in order to do that you will have to bring a letter from your employer.
It's their policy.

Below, you can compare top bank accounts and see what fits you best. I will mainly focus on things like cashback, interest rates and overdrafts as these are the most important factors. You can always change your bank if you're not satisfied with their service.

1. **Natwest Select Account**

Account fee & requirements	No monthly fee
Interest rate	0% AER
Arranged overdraft	£10 buffer, then £6 per month & 19.89% EAR variable

2. Barclays Bank Account

Account fee & requirements	No monthly fee
Interest rate	0% AER
Arranged overdraft	£15 buffer, then £3 per day

3. The Royal Bank Select Account

Account fee & requirements	No monthly fee
Interest rate	0% AER
Arranged overdraft	£15 buffer, then £6 per month & 19.89% EAR variable

4. Bank of Scotland Classic Account

Account fee & requirements	No monthly fee
Interest rate	0% AER
Arranged overdraft	1p per £7 overdrawn per day

5. B Current

Account fee & requirements	No monthly fee
Interest rate	0.5% AER (on up to £2,000)
Arranged overdraft	£10 buffer, then £6 per month & 12.5% EAR variable

6. HSBC Basic Bank Account

Account fee & requirements	No monthly fee
Interest rate	0% AER
Arranged overdraft	£10 buffer

As you can see, holding a bank account itself is free of charge. So if I were you and wanted a traditional bank account it would be HSBC, Natwest or Barclays. This is an opinion from most people I know in the UK.

However, if you're more like me and aren't fond of traditional banking

Ever since we discovered online banking, we don't want to be a part of a traditional bank anymore. Only where it is an absolute must. For instance, my boyfriend uses a credit card, not because he needs to but because using it in a right way effects his credit score which will become useful when trying to get a good deal on mortgage.

Soon after we arrived to UK, we heard about Revolut and Monzo, two powerful online banks that are spreading worldwide with lightspeed.

It's easier to send bank transfers that arrive instantly no matter what day or hour it is, the banks operate 24/7.

Revolut - It's very simple to register, you download the app, order a card (which arrives quickly to your address), make a safe account and you have your bank all ready.

The best part of this is there are no fees for being a part of it; I only had to pay £5 to order a card. Another great thing is you can simply split your money into different currencies without paying for an exchange fee. A little bit of one currency and a little bit of another... Whenever and wherever you travel, the currency you need is available in seconds with no additional FX price.

This is perfect for those who travel a lot.

More about Revolut on their website https://www.revolut.com/.

Monzo – is more appropriate for use inside UK but you can use it anywhere, and it is so much better than traditional banking.
If you lose your card, freeze it in your app and get a new one the next day. (Or defrost it if you find it again.)

More about Monzo on their website https://monzo.com/.

Revolut is better for travel and Monzo is better when in UK.

Monzo charges 3% for cash withdraws over £200.

Revolut charges 2% for cash withdraws over £200.

You don't have to decide which one is good for you. You can simply have both as we do.

Both banks also have an option for Premium account which is payable on a monthly basis. Personally, we don't need premium accounts because we don't make large cash withdraws. If you're used to paying online or paying by card you'll be fine.

I also have a Revolut Business account for my self-employment income (as a sole trader you will need a separate business account).

EDIT April 2021: I am switching from Revolut to Starling account (personal and business) since I just found it operates much better than Revolut.

#6 PHONE NUMBER

You will, of course, need a British phone number as soon as possible after you move to the UK.

There are five UK mobile companies that provide service for UK mobile phone users: EE, Three, O2 and Vodafone. These have the widest coverage in the country.

EE has the best nationwide coverage and its 4G download speeds are far in excess of those available from rival networks. It was also stated to have the best coverage in the London Underground. Vodafone was named the worst phone network.

Three stands out for its comprehensive international roaming scheme, Go Roam, that allows you to use your phone in up to 60 locations for no extra charge. Three was our choice, and we are pleased with their terms for now.

I use Three's Pay As You Go. It's very simple for me because there is no monthly plan and I recevied a free SIM. All I had to do was top-up a small amount of credit which was around £10 (GBP). Calls are 10p per minute, a text is also 10p and mobile data is only 5p/MB. I don't use my phone much other than wi-fi and receiving calls from my clients so I haven't even got to the half of my credit in four months. I think these £10 will last me more than half a year which is unbelievably cheap.

My friend, for instance, is on an O2 Pay As You Go tariff, which is £15/month for 1000 texts, 500 minutes, and 5GB of data with rollover. She can also use her mobile data in a number of European countries at no cost, unlike US carriers that charge daily fees.

If you want more details on UK mobile providers, you can check out https://www.techadvisor.co.uk.

#7 NATIONAL INSURANCE

Make sure to apply to national insurance as soon as you arrive to the UK. You can always do that later, because I know plenty of people that started working without it if they could prove to have a right to work in the UK.

Another reason to take care of it as soon as possible is because the tax deducted from your salary is slightly higher until you receive a permanent National Insurance Number (NIN).

Considering you're moving from the US you'll have a Biometric residence permit (BRP). Good chances are, you'll already have the NIN printed on the back of your BRP.

If you don't, you must apply for one if you plan to work, apply for a student loan or claim benefits. You can only apply if you're in the UK.

All information regarding applying for a NIN can be found on https://www.gov.uk/apply-national-insurance-number

Just make sure you call them from a UK telephone number and that you stay in the UK from the moment you call until the appointment. Don't worry about it too much, say that you're in the country and tell them you're not leaving the UK before the appointment. This was very important to them. Ask them what is it that you need to bring with you. (Face-to-face appointments are currently not required because of coronavirus.)

After the appointment, you'll receive a temporary NIN while waiting for the permanent one (it usually takes up to 6 weeks but it can take up to 16 weeks in the time of coronavirus).

#8 DRIVING LICENCE

If you already have a driving license from your previous country of residence, you can exchange it for a British one.
Just follow this link: https://www.gov.uk/exchange-foreign-driving-licence.

You'll want to do this eventually because the car insurance will cost you more if you don't own a British license.

#9 TAXES

It will not be easy when it comes to taxes while living in the UK as a US citizen.

You probably already know this fact but all US citizens are required to file a US tax return no matter where they live. The United States is among only a few governments who tax international income earned by their citizens, as well as permanent residents, residing overseas.

If you're moving to the UK from the US, there's good news and bad news.

The good news is that the US and UK have a tax treaty that allows you to deduct your UK taxes from what you'd owe in the US. You can read all the crazy details in here if you want to dive completely into it - https://www.gov.uk/government/publications/usa-tax-treaties.

The best way you can protect your income from double taxation is called The Foreign Earned Income Exclusion. It is the largest tax advantage available to you as an expat. If elected, your first (appx.) $100,000 earned overseas is exempt from income tax, unless you are an employee of the US government.

In order to qualify, you'll have to meet one of the following two criteria:

- 1) Work full time inside a foreign country for an entire calendar year - known as the **Bona Fide Residence Test**
- 2) Work outside of the United States for at least 330 of any 365 day period - known as the **Physical Presence Test**

This is again, a huge pile of information (as I said - this is sadly a complicated part of moving), so I suggest you read more about it here - https://www.irs.gov/individuals/international-taxpayers/foreign-earned-income-exclusion.

There are exceptions to the rule of course, because nothing about US taxes is ever simple. US expats earning investment income, for example, will owe tax on the profits.

What about self-employed expats?

Americans who are self-employed, sole traders, or running their own business are typically responsible for paying the self-employment tax in the United States, even if they are utilizing the foreign earned income exclusion to shelter their British earnings from US tax.

But there's a way to work around it. US expats, who are paying into and covered by the National Insurance, can be exempt from paying the self-employment tax. This strategy is made possible by the Social Security Totalization Agreement between the U.S. and the U.K.

So what's the bad news?

The bad news is that there are additional US tax forms for citizens living abroad, including the FBAR for foreign bank accounts. It can get quite complicated so better do your homework and take the time gathering all the necessary information about it in advance. Doing everything last minute is nerv-wrecking, trust me.
Depending on your financial situation, you may end up paying several thousand dollars to a professional to ensure your taxes are done right. I suggest you hire a dual UK / US expat tax firm to handle your tax returns, although it will cost a couple of thousand dollars (around 2000 USD).

It's just the way it is so I hope that doesn't discourage you from making that important step in your life.

"Move out of your comfort zone. You can only grow if
you are willing to feel awkward
and uncomfortable when you
try something new."

- Brian Tracy

#10 IMPORTANT WEBSITES

To summarize all that's been written above plus some more, I am going to fill this part with essential links of all the websites you need to visit for more information.

There is still much more to learn when you're ready to go dive into details. Just don't become overwhelmed, make one step at a time and everything is going to be fine.

I've put this together all in one place, so you don't feel lost and don't have to look for everything by yourself.

JOB SEARCH and BUSINESS	www.indeed.jobs
	www.linkedin.com (*app)
	www.gov.uk
	www.totaljobs.com
INSURANCE	www.comparethemarket.com
BANKING	www.revolut.com (*app)
	www.monzo.com (*app)
	https://www.starlingbank.com/
	www.hsbc.co.uk www.personal.natwest.com https://www.barclays.co.uk/
PROPERTY	www.rightmove.co.uk
	www.zoopla.co.uk
VISA, NATIONAL INSURANCE, DRIVING LICENSE, RESIDENCY, ADDRESS	www.gov.uk
HEALTH SERVICE	www.nhs.uk
TRANSPORTATION	www.thetrainline.com (*app) https://liftshare.com/uk
SECOND-HAND (ITEMS, CARS, PROPERTIES)	www.gumtree.com

#11 DEDUCTIONS FROM YOUR PAY

- **INCOME TAX:**

Most people in the UK get a Personal Allowance tax-free income. This is the amount of income you can have before you pay tax. The standard Personal Allowance is £12,570, which is the amount of income you don't have to pay tax on.

Band	Taxable income	Tax rate
Personal Allowance	Up to £12,570	0%
Basic rate	£12,571 to £50,270	20%
Higher rate	£50,271 to £150,000	40%
Additional rate	over £150,000	45%

Super simple example:

Let's say you earned **£1500 of taxable income** this month (without food and travel expense, which is non-taxable).
Subtract approx. £1047.50 (which is a non-taxable allowance on a monthly basis):

$$£1500 - £1047.50 = £452.50$$

Take 20% of the amount left:

$$0.2 \times £452.50 = £90.50$$

This is the tax you pay this month.
But note this: if your annual salary adds up to **£12.570 or less** by the end of the tax year, you get a **full refund of all the tax** that you paid in certain months.

The current tax year is from 6 April 2021 to 5 April 2022.

*You can also apply for Income Tax Reliefs if you're eligible for them. You can find that out on https://www.gov.uk/income-tax-reliefs

Basically, all details are provided on www.gov.uk website, when the time comes to dive into them. I've only gatheres the crucial elements and made them simple so you can understand the basics of the UK system.

- **NATIONAL INSURANCE (NI):**

You pay National Insurance if you're 16 or over and either:

- an employee earning above £184 a week
- self-employed and making a profit of £6,515 or more a year

It means that you pay NI if your monthly pay as an employee exceeds £737. Anything above it, you'll have to take 12% from it to calculate your national insurance.

Your pay	Class 1 National Insurance rate
£184.01 to £967 a week	12%
Over £967 a week	2%

Super simple example:

So, let's say you earned £1500 of taxable income this month. Subtract £737 from it:

$$£1500 - £737 = £763$$

Now, let's calculate 12% of the remained:

$$0.12 \times £763 = \mathbf{£91.56}$$

This is the amount you would have to pay toward your NI if you earned £1500. Like I said, very simple.

You can pay less in special circumstances for instance if you're a married woman or widow or you have more than one job.

National Insurance is deducted by your employer each month before you get paid.

#12 GROCERIES AND SHOPPING

The most popular UK supermarkets are Waitrose, Marks & Spencer, Aldi, Lidl, Morrisons, Iceland, Sainsbury's, Tesco, Asda.

In the recent survey, customers were asked to rate stores and online operations based on their experience in the past six months on categories such as quality, value for money, service from delivery drivers, how easy it was to find products, and whether shoppers would recommend it to a friend.

Waitrose was first, M&S came in second, Lidl and Aldi shared the third place.

We personally love Lidl and Aldi the most because of their affordable prices since we are living frugal and use all of our savings for investing. But of course, we are satisfied with their products as well. Not only groceries but they also have an enormous offer of goods, excellent offer of clothing, sports equipment, and kitchen accessories. We also went grocery shopping in Tesco many times as well as Morrisons but couldn't see any difference in product quality. We did see a difference in price though.

Other reason we like to shop in Lidl is that it is the closest grocery store in our area. And to be honest, we hate spending too much time on buying food. It's just something we gotta do to get some food. We rather spend our time in growing a business, reading a book or taking a walk in the park.

Lidl has also launched their Too Good To Waste 5kg Vegetable boxes for £1.50 which is awesome for frugal people like us. I also hate food going to waste and do everything to save as much as I can.

If you like to shop online, I would recommend Amazon UK. We bought almost everything we need for our apartment (kitchen appliances, office chairs, lamps, etc.) on Amazon.

When buying used second-hand stuff, especially used furniture, you can use Gumtree (the UK equivalent of Craigslist) and Salvation Army. They are the leading website in the UK for shopping various items, used cars and apartments.
IKEA is another affordable new option. We bought all of our furniture there and we're super happy with it.

We usually buy clothes and other related accesories in Primark. It's very affordable and their offer is way larger than one needs.

But when we want totally inexpensive cute and small home accesories we don't mind going to Poundland or Poundstretcher. I mean come on, can it get any cheaper than that? This is just to buy something nice, not feel guilty about it and then when we get tired of it, we can just give it away on Gumtree or Facebook give-away groups.

These are just some of my favorite options but you'll find what suits you. Just don't settle for the first you run into. It's always nice and fun to do a little bit of a research by yourself, especially if you're not in a rush to buy something.

#13 SELF-EMPLOYMENT

It's super easy to start your own business in the UK, even if you already have a full-time job. UK is a country with great business environment and if you know what you are doing, you could easily run a successful business. You can **register as a sole trader** in the UK without any cost and it's just a 30 minute process on the gov.uk website.

All you need to do is fill in your basic information, name your business (be careful not to use trademarks) and the date of starting. And let's not forget to say something about what type your business is.

You won't have to pay anything for being a self-employed person except **taxes after the end of the tax-year** (you'll have plenty of time to do that). This is called filing a **Self Assessment tax return**.

You will probably need to pay **National Insurance**. But all of that depends on how much you earn, or should I say how much profit you gain. If, for instance, your partner works a full-time job and let's say you start a service based business as a sole trader (tutoring, proofreading,...). You earn a decent but part-time income, chances are you won't have to pay any of that, nor taxes nor National Insurance. Because in order to pay that, you'll need to reach a certain profit over a one year period.

What (and how much) you pay as a self-employed person:

1. NATIONAL INSURANCE

You usually pay two types of National Insurance if you're self-employed:

Class 2: if your profits reach £6,515 or more a year.
Class 4: if your profits are £9,569 or more a year.

Class	Rate for tax year 2019 to 2020
Class 2	£3.05 a week
Class 4	9% on profits between £9,569 and £50,270 2% on profits over £50,270

self-employed income – your expenses = your profit

2. INCOME TAX

Good news is that the first £12,570 of your income is non-taxable. It is called a Personal Allowance. It is the same if you're employed working for someone else.
Everything that is above this amount, take 20% of it as your income tax.
And all the profit that is above £50,270 is taxed 40%. When you reach profit this high then it's definitely time to stop being self-employed and start a Limited Company instead.

Do you want to be self-employed in the UK?

This link will take you step-by-step:

https://www.gov.uk/set-up-self-employed

#14 PEOPLE AND LIFESTYLE

Well, the weather's nice!

No, not exactly. I wish for more sunny days here. I am very much used to having more of them.

There can be days or even weeks with mostly satisfying and mostly sunny weather but if I'm totally honest, showers are definitely more frequent than the clear blue sky.

I say showers instead of rain because the usual weather isn't rainy as much as it is showery and windy. This is the actual problem here in the UK. And the fact that air is generally humid. Even if it is sunny it can be quite windy often. Sometimes the clearer the sky is the windier it is.

I must say that summer of 2019 was extremely and surprisingly sunny and hot which was awesome for everyone.

Bottom line is, there will be good days and bad ones. You'll just have to use those good ones to enjoy and be outside as much as you can. Seriously, make the most out of each day.

Take advantage of those bad days as well. Clean your house and organize your household, read books or watch movies you haven't seen and be lazy without feeling guilty for it. Or go to a nice quiet coffee shop, order a hot drink and read a book. Or take a walk in the rain. Why not?

The lifestyle here is pretty much going to the shopping centers and visiting pubs when having a free time. People love to go to pubs. I don't but I see this is the case here. This is not the kind of lifestyle we personally have. It's not exactly our cup of tea. ☺

We don't want to waste so much of our time shopping and sitting in a pub. But we do like to enjoy coffee outside on a nice day whether it is at home or in a coffee shop. Grabbing a beer in a local pub from time to time is great and all, just not too often. We much rather go to a park or you know, we have our hobbies.

In the end, it's all up to your interests. Parks and natural reserves are beautiful in the UK. I recommend visiting them as much as you can.

Beside other sports (like runnning and gym) we live in a place where archery is pretty common. So this is a fun idea you should look into when you arrive to the UK.

Just don't be surprised when you see that people here are generally not so much into sports except running or football. They work all day throughout the week and on weekends they do shopping or stay at home.

It's sad to see that they are not enjoying life as they could. And should.

But they do enjoy watching football very much (the same as soccer in the US). When the game is on, you'll see over-crowded pubs everywhere.

So I guess we all have something of our own to enjoy in.

#15 TRANSPORTATION

Let me tell you one thing first.

Buying and having a car isn't cheap, I know that. You will have to pay for insurance which can be quite high as I already mentioned before, especially as a beginner driver in the UK (even if you have years of experience in other country, it doesn't count). You start at zero in the UK. Insurance will go down over the years.

Even fuel (such as gas or diesel) is priced high in the UK.

And did I mention that most UK employers don't pay for the travel cost? In Europe it is common that people have travel expenses covered so they don't pay for travel themselves. Well, in the UK, all travel expenses will probably be covered by you. So living near your workplace is essential.

But still. Regardless of everything, having your own car is a bliss compared to having to use public transportation all the time. You get to decide when and where you can go so you don't have too look at all kinds of schedules. Everything is just prefect except for the traffic.

UK is a highly populated country. So it's not a surprise that during the rush hour being stuck in the traffic day after day is a huge pain in the ass.

Public transport (such as tram or underground) is mostly over-crowded in every large city. Many times you won't get a chance to sit down. What I would suggest is taking a bus in that case. At least you'll be able to sit on your way home. And I think if I am going to be stuck on the road anyway, atleast I don't have to be the driver so I can close my eyes or read a book or write an article in the meantime. It's a time used productively. For me, time is the most important thing. So even the thought of spending two hours daily in traffic while having to watch the road all the time makes me nervous.

Another suggestion is going to work with your bicycle. I take bicycle whenever I can, depending on the weather forecast. Rain is usually quite soft in England so even if it's raining a little bit you don't need an umbrella. People are so used to it here that I rarely see anyone with an umbrella while it is gently raining.

What about trains? They can be quite expensive if you use them to travel to work. But they are the best idea for going on a trip that is far away. You'll save a lot of your time and nerves becaus train ride is so much safer, faster and much more relaxing.

For instance, train from Nottingham to Luton airport (which is about 1.5 hour drive) can cost anywhere between £30 (only at certain hours) to a ridiculous price of £100. The types of ticket fares in UK:

- **Anytime**
- **Off-peak**
- **Super off-peak**
- **Advance**

It's recommendable to always buy a ticket before boarding the train and keep it to yourself because there is usually a conductor or a sort of inspector who may charge you a fine if you don't have it.

The bus prices are much more affordable comparing to train transport on some routes but may cost the same as a train ride or even more on certain routes. So do your homework and always check different options to get the best price possible.

Trams aren't that expensive if you use it occasionally. One adult ticket is £1.40 which doesn't sound much.

But, if you travel daily to work and back - even if it's just a short ride - it can cost you about £60/month which is a lot for only a tram ride. Now if you travel by train and tram (my boyfriend had to use both at first until we got a car) it's hell of a lot to pay on a monthly basis.
Another thing I would strongly suggest is Liftshare. It is a website where you can find or offer a lift on a certain destination on a certain day, for an affordable price.

So if you're traveling somewhere with your own car, you can offer a lift to one or few people and save a few bucks here and there. If you want to go somewhere and don't have a ride or don't feel like driving, go find if there is anyone going in that direction. They saved me a lot of times, especially at the beginning. Not to mention I've met some pretty nice people whi became my regular 'drivers' since I don't like to drive in the UK (for now).

So what now?

1. Find a place to live near your work place. Employers in the UK don't pay for your travel expenses as they do in many other countries.

2. Take a bus to work.

3. Ride a bike. It's healthy.

4. Walk as much as you can. It's healthy.

5. Buy yourself a small economycal car.

6. Travel by sharing a lift with another person, whethet it's for work or any other reason. Plus it's fun and you'll meet a lot of great people on the way.

So, now you've seen and read all the most important steps towards your new life in the UK. Hopefully, you'll get throught them as easy as possible and that this book helps you on your way.

I might have missed something that is important to you personally or the certain rules have changed in the meantime after writing this guide. Let's just be optimistic that not much did change and that this short guide serves you as a good starting point, if not more. This book was written from a very frugal point of view. Maybe you're not a frugal type or don't want to be. That's okay, do what you believe it's best for you. We believe frugal tips are generally useful at the beginning of a new life in another country but it doesn't have to be like that for everyone.

However it is in your case, we wish you all the best.

Happy planning,

happy moving and

a beautiful life of course! ☺

Made in United States
North Haven, CT
05 February 2024